Alan Stanley

Love Lyrics

Alan Stanley

Love Lyrics

ISBN/EAN: 9783744776325

Printed in Europe, USA, Canada, Australia, Japan

Cover: Foto ©Thomas Meinert / pixelio.de

More available books at **www.hansebooks.com**

CONTENTS

LOVE LYRICS

AT EVENING

How quickly sinks the westering sun
In heavens of opal hue ;
Ere day dies, eve has well begun
To cast her shadows blue
Down on the city at our feet
O'er tree, and grove and valley sweet
Which Arno wanders through.

And you are silent, love, this hour
This last flushed hour of day—
Is it because my love's strong power

A

Has drawn your soul away?
Do you regret your love of me?
Does your soul struggle to be free
Flutter and fail alway?

The sun has gone, the lights appear
Along each sinuous street,
The sky as one vast gem is clear,
Night's first frail breeze is sweet
With scent of flowers, that close to sleep
And through the night their bloom to keep
Till roused by morning's feet.

Do your lips tremble now to mine?
In your eyes can I see
Spring up a light of love divine,
A new born ecstasy?
Ah, dear, I shiver 'neath your kiss,
Have I not waited long for this—
That you should turn to me?

The nightingale in yonder grove,

Lifts up his voice in praise,

He knows and chants our lyric-love,

The love that never stays.

He sings ' This moment is supreme

Yet fleeting as a fitful gleam,

Nor comes in after days.'

TO A CHILD

My heart's desire is white and fair,
More gold than sunshine is his hair,
And in his hazel eyes I see
Such tender looks well up for me,
That I forget my former care.

So frail he is, so slim and rare,
A willow wand he seems to be
That quivers with each passing air,
     —My heart's desire.

His beauty fills me with despair,
It overwhelms me so ; I dare

TO A CHILD

Scarcely to pray on bended knee

That I may kiss him reverently,

Fearing to stain beyond repair

My heart's desire.

ERRATA

Page 15, line 10, for 'grow' read 'glow'

,, 17, ,, 6, ,, 'irer' ,, 'iris'

,, 32, ,, 6, ,, 'words',, 'chords'

LOVE IN AUTUMN

WHEN Autumn shades creep o'er the sky,
And flowers and fruits are rich and red,
The birds spread out their wings to fly.

The leaves fall from the tree-tops high
And brown upon the walks are spread,
When autumn shades creep down the sky.

The gaunter branches creak and cry
Knocking and twisting overhead,
And shivering birds prepare to fly.

The winds are growing cold and dry,
All nature knows the summer dead—
Now sombre shades creep down the sky.

My heart grows weary and I sigh
For golden glories that are fled—
—Even the birds prepare to fly.

The low wind moans a lullaby,
My loved one comes with gentle tread.
Still leaden is the Autumn sky
And frightened birds spread wings and fly.

THE OLD STORY

You loved me, sweet, and I loved you,
Each of us deemed the other true—
What was it fell between us two?

Your mouth a crimson flower to me,
Your eyes an unsung melody
Woven to which I fain would be.

Each unto each we were complete,
No sound unto my ears was sweet
As the soft echo of your feet.

Was it because we loved too well,
We tired and broke the fervid spell?
Wearied of heaven, longed for hell?

THE OLD STORY

I know not, and I do not fret,
Because I hear that you forget
Even that we have ever met.

Yes, I remember without pain,
Our joy in sunshine and in rain,
And only sigh to love again.

SURRENDER

YOUR life was in its spring time when we met,
The flowers bent down in homage as you came
Whispering of love ; I never could forget,
Once having seen, that body white of thine,
Or dear gold hair crowned with the purple vine,
And crimson mouth which set my blood a-flame.

You threw around me chains of lilies white,
You tangled me within your golden hair,
And made me drunken with the sweet delight
Of violet eyes, in whose mysterious shade
I loved to gaze, entranced yet half afraid,
On that shy soul, as thy fair body fair.

Let all men shudder, let them turn aside

And mocking point whene'er I tread the street.

You are my very life, it is my pride

To have this bright shame writ upon my brow

And to possess thee, recking nothing now

If for one moment our two souls may meet.

A DREAM

Last night I dreamed in mid-most sleep
My love came to my lonely bed,
And threw white arms about my head,
And kissed mine eyes too tired to weep.

White arms were thrown about my head,
And I felt subtle fingers twine
Within these tresses brown of mine,
Yet still I lay as one half-dead.

But when I felt warm kisses fall
On upturned throat and barren breast,
Then stirred I with a wild unrest
To know the sweetest kiss of all.

AT MONACO

THE waves upon the low beach play,
A silver moon sails o'er the sea,
Upon the cliff in stately row
The lights of the casino glow,
While far away
The band sighs forth a melody.

O come, beloved, unto me
And lean your cheek again on mine,
For love is in the air to-night,
And you are made for my delight,
So let it be,
If only I be made for thine.

THE DAWN NOCTURNE

(AUGUST BLUE)

SILVER mists on a silver sea,
And white clouds overhead
Sailing the grey sky speedily
To where the east turns red.
And one lone boat her sails has spread,
Sails of the whitest lawn,
That seem to listen for the tread
Of the tender feet of dawn.

The risen sun now makes the sky
An arching roof of gold,
Amber the clouds turn as they fly
Uncurling fold on fold;

The sun a goblet seems to hold
A draught of fervid wine,
And the young day no longer cold
Glows with a fire divine.

Stripped for the sea your tender form
Seems all of ivory white,
Through which the blue veins wander warm
O'er throat and bosom slight,
And as you stand, so slim, upright
The glad waves grow and yearn
To clasp you circling in their might,
To kiss with lips that burn.

Flashing limbs in the waters blue
And gold curls floating free ;
Say, does it thrill you through and through
With ardent love, the sea ?
A very nymph you seem to be
As you glide and dive and swim,

While the mad waves clasp you fervently
Possessing every limb.

King of the Sea, triumphant boy,
Nature itself made thrall
To God's white work without alloy
On whom no stain doth fall.
Gaze on him, slender, fair, and tall,
And on the yearning sea
Who deigns to creep and cling, and crawl,
His worshipper to be.

NOW DIES THE SUN

Now dies the sun and all the sky is red
With his outflowing life blood ; one by one
The sleepy flowers droop a languid head,—
Now dies the sun.

Along the wall the slanting shadows run
And quiver through the golden irir-bed,
While warning birds proclaim that day is done.

Lo ! the pale moon by gentle breezes led
Drifts like a wraith, ere night has yet begun,
All grows so hushed, the very world seems dead,—
Now dies the sun.

B

AN OLD PICTURE

It hangs alone upon the panelled wall,
A faded picture in a faded frame,
No traces are there of the artist's name,
For each year as it stole into the hall
Crept o'er the writing with its dusty feet,
And Time upon the pale Madonna's face
A veil has thrown, through which we dimly trace
Eyes of deep blue by sorrow made more sweet.

Perchance in bygone years in Tuscany
Where maize-fields redden to the autumn sun
The Painter watched the slanting shadows run
Over the city walls, and learned from him,
The mystic Botticelli, how to limn
The Virgin's face ablaze with ecstasy.

A NIGHT CLUB AND A VALSE

DRAW back the curtains, let the dawn come in
And let new daylight mingle with the light
Of candles that have guttered through the night,
Of flaring gas-jets in this haunt of sin.

The sleepy orchestra begins a tune,
'Tis the last valse and you with languid smile
Renew your well-worn witchery, and guile
Of eyes that 'neath their painted lashes swoon.

O how the music pulses, rises, calls,
On tremulous strings of ill-tuned violins,
Whispering of agonies and aching sins,
And a wild longing o'er my spirit falls;

For as like spectres we two move along
My mouth upon your mouth, the music seems
A memory exquisite of dying dreams
Which in my brain beats forth this dancing song.

    Ah darling, daylight is not for us twain;
For us the darkness and the biting pain
Of love that hate becomes, yet yearning still
Drinks deep of passion, and may never fill
The aching void of longing. Come, once more
Let us glide swiftly o'er the polished floor
To the mad music of the Toréador.
And let our feet trip as with frenzy fired,
For both our hearts are breaking and so tired
That we would fain fall to a lasting sleep
With eyes so weary that they may not weep.
O that we two upon the last sweet strain
Might drift away ! nor ever know again
Joy's cloying dulness, or sin's wearing pain.

FROM NORTH TO SOUTH

(SAPPHO TO ALCÆUS)

THE South is fair and the North is bleak ;
Ah me, how I long to be there,
And through the vines my love to seek
And to touch with my hands his golden hair,
For the North is bleak and the South is fair.

Ah, bleak is the North and the South is fair,
And I long for my lover's mouth,
That kissing him I might lose my care,
For my love is fair as the fragrant South,
And wine-red is his red red mouth,
And gold as sun-set his golden hair.

O, my spirit flies from the North ice-bound,
It wings and flutters unto the South,
Nor will it stay, till it has found
A resting-place on his lithe keen mouth,
Or nestles against his fervid heart,

　　Sinking to rest
　　On his warm white breast,
　　To sleep, and ne'er to part.

And my body yearns to follow my soul,
And my lips his lips to seek,
For though all the world from Pole to Pole
Lay between us, yet my soul
Would seek his soul; though the flesh be weak
I long to follow my fluttering soul.

For the South is fair and the North is bleak,
And I know my true love wanders there,
And twines the vine leaves in his hair,
And crushes the grape against his mouth;

Nor does he know my fretting care,

As he wanders blithe and debonair.

But O, how I long and yearn to be there,

For the North is bleak and the South is fair.

LOVE AT HINKSEY

In the grey city at our feet
The lights gleam out, and one by one
Each gas-jet makes a mimic sun
Now the real sun has set, and sweet
The air grows with the heavy scent
Each flowering bush of May has lent;
The sky above a clear-cut gem,
And the moon rising from the sea
Trailing her white robes silently,
Has seven stars for a diadem.

When the sun set the breeze, too, fell,
Fluttering down like a wounded bird,
Now only its dying call is heard
From where wan river waters swell,

Amid tall lilies golden grown
We two in silence stand alone.
Your trembling hand in mine is prest,
I know within your sweet grey eyes
Love lights a torch which never dies
But flares for ever in unrest.

Ah dear, you love me now, and yet
Have I not often felt despair
Lest I should never touch your hair,
Or that our lips had never met?
I thought that you would never be
More than a simple friend to me.
Have I not known you two long years?
Have I not striven to make you love?
I think some angel from above
Has moved you by my aching tears.

You are a perfect poem, sweet,
Sung to an angel's melody

Before the Throne in ecstasy,

Where choir to choir the song repeat

Through all the columned courts of Heaven.

Dear God to you such grace has given,

Has wrought you as a golden flower,

Has made you as a purple star,

Or as a drifting nenuphar,

Or as a wondrous ivory tower.

Far in the hush of that young corn

Where only birds and flowers may see,

You shall be all in all to me,

And we will rest there till the morn

Turns emerald-sky to ruby red

And crowns with gold your golden head.

And lends unto your eyes new fire,

And makes your splendid, curving mouth

A gorgeous poppy of the South

Culled for some God's desire.

A REQUIEM

GOD took her when she was so young,
So young and fair,
She seemed a flower to beauty sprung
When spring is rare
With primrose and with violet,
And daisies for a coronet.

She lingered here so short a space
Of fleeting years,
Knew summer's sunshine, autumn's grace,
And winter's tears,
Then withered swiftly, ah so soon!
Frail spring flower born to die in June!

And yet maybe, 'tis better so
Better for me,
To drain at once the dregs of woe
And then be free.
If she had lived in after years
She might have scorned my aching tears.

So by her grave I will not weep
Though she be dead,
But leave her to a lasting sleep
With one prayer said.
She loved me to the last, and I
Rejoice at that, yet needs must sigh
To say, ' Good-bye.'

AT BOURNEMOUTH

THE sun is bright, the waves laugh out
And break in foam upon the shore,
Above, the sea-gulls sweep and scream,
Their clear-cut pinions glance and gleam,
And oft above the breakers' roar
I hear the merry bathers shout.

From out the waves they leap and run
In freedom o'er the shimmering sand,
They laugh, and nature smiles to see
Youth's unrestrained hilarity.
Lo! gladness reigns along the land
And knows the kisses of the sun.

O could I join that happy throng,
And lose my care and laugh as they,
Or kiss the lips of one I love,
And rest within some shady cove
Where only tender shadows play
Lightly the lichened rocks along!

It may not be, I do not care
For spring, or sun, or sea,
I who have loved these things, now long
For crowded streets and busy throng,
Where my beloved last walked with me,
Where last I touched that golden hair.

TO A POET

You too have sung, but with a deeper note,
    Ah, not as I.
I, the poor song-bird from whose narrow throat
    Rings but a single cry.

I, the weak egoist, can of self but sing
    My joy, my pain,
To others my weak verses may but bring
    The same thought sung again.

But you from life's great varied lyre have made
    A chant more true,
On all its wires of gold most deftly played
    And fashioned them to you.

You sing your love with passionate sweet song,
     And yet you know
Life's tumult that goes hurrying along,
     Its ecstasies, its woe.

Where did you learn your mystic harmonies,
     Your subtle words,
Your tremulous heart-reaching melodies,
     Your splendid coloured words?

You, the true songster, smile but if you will
     At this my praise,
Yet keep your well-loved friendship for me still,
     Through life's long after days.

LOVE'S GIFTS

(A NOCTURNE)

LOVE lends a light unto your eyes,

A strange, new light,

It is a light that never dies,

Though long the night,

For ever in those eyes of thine,

Will flash the flame of love divine.

Love lends new gold unto your hair,

A strange, new gold,

It is a gold most bright and rare,

On strand and fold,

Nor will it ever grow less bright,

Though long the day and long the night.

C

Love lends new crimson to your mouth,

That perfect flower,

The crimson of the flushing south,

A wondrous dower

Of scarlet, splendid and complete,

Such gifts love makes to you, my sweet.

Your hair is all of wondrous gold,

And scarlet is

Your tender mouth, while white and cold

As moonlight's kiss

Your marble limbs, you seem to be

A harmony

Of crimson, ivory, and gold.

AN IDYLL AT MARSEILLES

I HARDLY dreamed as we walked together
Through the busy streets of the sea-girt town,
Charmed as we were by the sweet spring weather
And green leaves bursting from branches brown ;
I hardly dreamed on that young spring day
Of the infinite love you bore to me,
Happy and careless we strolled our way
Through the long, straight street to the sun-lit sea.

Yet as we sat in the late afternoon
On the pavement edging the café gay,
The touch of your hand came as a boon
And I did not draw my hand away.

The glance of your eyes as you looked to me
O'er the half-filled glass of your absinthe dim,
Seemed as the swish of my northern sea
That kindles the blood in the languid limb.

And as eve crept down and the night-time came
With stars that throbbed in the sky o'erhead,
We watched the moon with an argent flame
Crawl up the heavens with stealthy tread,
And all in a moment a thrill went through me
As your flower-like head sunk down on my breast,
With one long kiss you proclaimed you knew me
And our hearts beat together in wild unrest.

WRECKAGE

I LOOKED into my glass last night
To trace my beauty there,
How wan I seemed by candle light
I who had been so fair.

The thick brown hair was flecked with grey,
Mine eyes were seared with sin,
With bitter heart I turned away
And crept my bed within.

Oh God, dear God, my youth has fled,
What now remains for me?
A shattered love, a passion dead,
A half-wrought melody.

IN A NORTHERN TOWN

(TWO IMPRESSIONS)

I

THE gas-jets glow, the hawker cries his wares,
Cheap fish, cheap meat, old fruit; the hurrying
    crowd
Loiters a moment, jeers and laughs and stares.

Voices of children playing, ring aloud,
Poor waifs of sin, beneath the light that flares,
They jest, as yet, by wrong and shame unbowed.

'Tis Saturday night and as I hurry too
Along with the noisy crowd, I think of one

Who wanders careless 'neath a southern sun
And knows the olives green against the blue.

Saturday night and traffic has begun
In wares most shameless, women pray and sue
For what? oh God, it thrills me through and through
To see the wrong that man to man has done.

II

Thinking of one, I could not stoop so low
Although her face was fair, and her great eyes
Grew pleading as she begged me with her go.

Aye, she was fair, and all the fire that lies
Deep in man's heart began to burn and glow
In a white-heat of flame that never dies.

I stooped and kissed her lips, but lo, there rose
A visioned face that falling tears did stain,
And through my heart there shot a sudden pain,
As half aloud, I cried, ' my loved one knows.'

I turned away ! nor kissed her lips again,

Yet see her still in dreams; a gas-jet throws

A yellow light upon her face which glows

Like some drenched flower beneath the falling rain.

THE DAWN OF LOVE

(ON A PICTURE)

THE morn steals in, our revelry is done,

The wine lies spilled upon the marble floor,

How faded are our roses, one by one

Their poor brown leaves turn, twist, and fall away

Ashamed to face the searching light of day,

They who have bloomed one long night and no
more.

Our comrades round us sleep, o'ercome with wine,

We two are left awake, and strangely fair

Your face becomes, as o'er it light divine

Of dawning love creeps roseate and sweet.

Oh, let me fall and kiss your stainless feet

Or touch with tender hand your splendid hair.

Your eyes were lustrous, dear, as all the night
We talked of love, and dallied with our wine
Like some frail orchid culled for man's delight
Seemed your white body, as you half reclined
Upon my heart, with scarlet flowers entwined
In the bright meshes of that hair of thine.

And now they all lie sleeping, fiercer grows
The passion that so long has in me burned,
Oh! how your falling raiment doth disclose
Your neck's fine curvings to my ardent gaze,
And lo I falter as my hot mouth strays
In trembling kisses o'er your throat upturned.

Your wreath falls down, well, let the blossoms
    fade,
They matter not, the rose of love is sweet;
The morning birds sing out in the far glade
Raising a nuptial-song, for we are one,
And for our marriage-torch there comes the sun
Flaming through heaven, with swift ardent feet.

A CHANCE ENCOUNTER

HER room was dimly lighted, everywhere
Flowers seemed more beautiful because they died,
Thick velvet curtains did the windows hide,
And on the walls were mirrors tall and rare,
That she might see herself on every side
When shaking out the masses of her hair
Of gold most wondrous and beyond compare—
A fitting mantle for her beauty's pride.

'Twas in the crowded noisy music-hall
I met her walking with her wanton tread
And fickle turnings of her golden head,
And the quick glance she gave me seemed to fall
With force electric, thrilling as the call
Of plaintive music wailing for our dead.

A NIGHT THOUGHT

WITHIN the night I lie awake and cry
On you who loved me in the spring-time bright;
Weary I count the passing hours that die
            Within the night.

O what ailed Love that he should thus take flight,
And leave me where the fading roses lie,
In the drear garden of our dead delight?

But sometime as I sleepless moan and sigh,
Will you return to cheer my aching sight?
To kiss my lips, my falling tears to dry
            Within the night?

A TRAVELLER TO HIS LADY

TOGETHER we have roamed afar
With love as a sure guiding star,
And many lands have known together,
Summer and spring and winter weather,
All unto us their joys have given,
'Neath northern clime and southern heaven :
Is it then strange we fear to tell
The words that speak our last farewell.

O we have seen the glad sun rise
A crimson flash in morning's skies,
Piercing the gloomy shades that lie
Over Rome's fallen majesty.

At Naples when the world's asleep,
How sweet to hear the glad waves leap
In laughter 'neath the vessel's prow !
Do you not hear their laughter now ?

In Capri when the eve came down
With tender shadows blue and brown,
Standing where slim, straight olives are,
We two have traced the falling star.

And in Marseilles one long spring night,
We talked until the morning light,
Showed how our faces had grown wan
With brooding our strange love upon.

In many lands, on many seas
We two have learned love's mysteries,
Until we knew them through and through,
And I was all in all to you.

But now romance is o'er, and lo,
The callous world would have you go

To unknown cruel lands, and I
Stretch pleading hands with yearning cry.

The cruel world bids us to part,
Yet cannot take from me your heart,
And you within those unknown lands
May ne'er forget my clinging hands.
And yet I cannot bear to tell,
The words that speak our last farewell.

A TRAGEDY

The city seemed asleep that time
The cold December month crept in,
And whitened with its snow and rime
The hardened ground, and yet within
Our hearts their glowed a rosy flame
Of springlike warmth, though winter came.

We loved, and all around seemed gay
To our enchanted eyes, though cold
And keen the chilling winds would play
With autumn's leaves, so dead, so old,
For us the air with song was filled,
Though song and songbird now were stilled.

Through the long nights we two would sit
To tell our love, the well-worn tale,
Watching the fickle shadows flit,
O'er warm red walls and ceiling pale,
Your hand within my hands was prest,
Your head lay pillowed on my breast.

And yet you say I never knew
Nor cared to know your inmost soul,
I never looked you through and through
Nor all your secret fancies stole,
I knew your lips, your eyes, your hair,
But not the shy soul lurking there.

So you drift from me, O my sweet,
Still colder grows your glance each day,
Love flies us on his wingèd feet,
I plead, and yet he will not stay ;
With tear-dimmed eyes I watch his flight
Till daylight falters into night.

D

But sometimes with reluctant voice

We whisper the old words again,

Feigning the long hours to rejoice

In pleasures that have turned to pain,

And ghosts of our dead joys arise

And mock us with their weeping eyes.

TWO RISPETTI

I

O city of the lilies, from the north
I stretch my hands to you, and yearning cry
' Lo, it is spring, ah let me then go forth
Unto the south, before the lilies die.'

The fields are golden all with daffodils,
The new-red rose a perfume rare distils,
And when at night the crescent moon turns pale
The air grows vocal with the nightingale.

II

Here, far away, I sit and dream, and lo!
A scent of lilies fills the darkened room,

The Angelus rings out, a crimson glow
Of southern sunshine floods the northern gloom.

I hear a well-known voice, I touch a hand
With love I roam along the pleasant land,
We pause and kiss, where flowers spring to our feet
' A kiss in dreamland yet a kiss most sweet.'

LOVE'S SONG

LIFE is a song, because you love me, dear,

A song angelic struck from harps of gold,

Its mystic harmonies may ne'er grow old

Nor its glad merriment turn sad and drear,

For as your lips seek mine in tender kiss

Our two mouths grow together as one flower,

And naught to us the passing of the hour,

For each hour brings renewal of our bliss

   In life's sweet song.

I hold your hands and look into your eyes

And mark the violet glories sleeping there,

I bend and touch the splendour of your hair,

My joy grows manifold and never dies ;

We are as one, O God, let never care

As some wild discord, marring all, arise

   In life's sweet song.

TO G——

——

These poems are all of love, and you
Inspired them, sweet.
Your beauty thrilled me through and through;
As melody to viola
So was I tuned to you.
What else, fond lover, can I do
But lay these offerings at your feet—
These poor, frail flowers at your feet?

SIDNEY LANIER. Complete Poems. 8vo. Portrait, cloth gilt, gilt top, 7s. 6d. net.

PERCY PINKERTON. Adriatica. Foolscap 8vo. Frontispiece, tastefully bound. 5s. net. *Edition limited to 250 copies.*

THOMAS BAILEY ALDRICH. Complete Poems. Demy 8vo. Fine engraved Portrait and Illustrations, cloth extra, 6s.

CLINTON SCOLLARD. On Sunny Shores. Crown 8vo. Illustrated, cloth gilt, 5s.

THEODORE WRATISLAW. Caprices : Poems. Foolscap 8vo, tastefully bound in white, with design of tulips on side by Gleeson White. *Edition limited to 100 numbered copies on hand-made paper.* 5s. net.

ARTHUR CLARK KENNEDY. Erotica : Poems. Foolscap 8vo. Frontispiece, tastefully bound. 3s. 6d. net. *Edition limited to 250 copies on hand-made paper.*

WALT WHITMAN. Leaves of Grass. Being his Complete Poems. Demy 8vo, portrait, cloth, gilt top, 9s.

—— Complete Prose Works. Portrait, uniform with the above. 9s.

JAMES RUSSELL LOWELL. A Fable for Critics. Crown 8vo, cloth, 5s. An Edition for the Book-lover, with 26 outline Portraits of the Authors mentioned in the Poem, and a Facsimile in Colour of the Rhyming Title-Page of the First Edition

—— The Vision of Sir Launfal. Crown 8vo. Eight charming phorogravures by E. H. Garrett, and portrait of Lowell in 1842 with long curls and deep linen collar, tastefully bound, 6s net.

A. ERNEST HINSHELWOOD. Through Starlight to Dawn. Second Edition. Crown 8vo, *printed on hand-made paper at the Chiswick Press*, sewed, 1s 6d ; cloth extra, gilt, 3s 6d.

JOHN KEATS, ROSES OF ROMANCE, FROM THE POEMS OF JOHN KEATS. One vol. 18mo. Frontispiece, 8 plates, and several beautiful head and tail pieces, by E. H. Garrett.

SHELLEY, PERCY BYSSHE. Flowers of Fancy. Selected from the Works of Percy Bysshe Shelley. One vol. 18mo. Frontispiece, 11 plates, and several beautiful head and tail pieces, by E. H. Garrett. *The two volumes are uniformly bound in light blue cloth, gilt extra, and boxed, price 7s 6d net. the set.* Gems selected by the Artist for his labour of love.

www.ingramcontent.com/pod-product-compliance
Lightning Source LLC
Chambersburg PA
CBHW031752090426
42739CB00008B/980